LIFE IN THE
CITIES

Written by **Sally Morgan**

Consultant: Keith Jones, BA
Environmental Consultant

PRINCETON ■ LONDON

Published in the United States and Canada by
Two-Can Publishing LLC
234 Nassau Street
Princeton, NJ 08542

www.two-canpublishing.com

© 2000 Two-Can Publishing

For information on Two-Can books and multimedia,
call 1-609-921-6700, fax 1-609-921-3349, or visit our web site at
http://www.two-canpublishing.com

'Two-Can' is a trademark of Two-Can Publishing.
Two-Can Publishing is a division of Zenith Entertainment plc,
43-45 Dorset Street, London W1H 4AB

hc ISBN 1-58728-5509
sc ISBN 1-58728-5657

hc 1 2 3 4 5 6 7 8 9 10 02 01 00
sc 1 2 3 4 5 6 7 8 9 10 02 01 00

Printed in Hong Kong

Photograph credits:
pp4-5 Tony Stone Worldwide/Robin Smith p7 (top) Britstock-IFA/Bern Ducke p7 (bottom) Tony Stone Worldwide p8 Image Bank/Wendy Chan
p9 (top) Zefa/K H Oster p9 (bottom) Britstock-IFA/Bern Ducke p11 (top) NHPA/Stephen Dalton p11 (bottom) Frank Lane Picture Agency/S Kaslowski p12 (top) Oxford
Scientific Films/Raymond J C Cannon p12 (bottom) Bruce Coleman/Erwin & Peggy Bauer p13 Bruce Coleman/Michael Freeman
p14 (top) Oxford Scientific Films/George I Bernard p14 (bottom) NHPA/Anthony Bannister p15 Frank Lane Picture Agency/F Polking p16 NHPA/
David Woodfall p17 Panos/Penny Tweedie pp18-19 Image Bank/Benn Mitchell p19 (top) NHPA/Michael Leach p20 (top) Oxford Scientific Films/
Stan Osolinski p21 (top) Science Photo Library/Dr Jeremy Burgess p21 (bottom) NHPA/David Woodfall pp22-23 Britstock-IFA/F Aberham
p23 (top) Image Bank/D S Henderson.

Front cover: Tony Stone Worldwide/Mark Feagal Back cover: NHPA/Stephen Dalton

Illustrations by Julie Carpenter. Story by Pauline Lalor. Story illustration by Brent Linley, The Inkshed.

CONTENTS

All words marked in **bold** can be found in the glossary.

LOOKING AT CITIES

Cities are built **environments** where many people live grouped together in one area. They were first built over 10,000 years ago, to offer safety and a chance for people to **trade**. Since then, they have grown much larger. They now have huge **populations**, often in the millions. People live and work in towering buildings or in the large areas of housing which are usually found in the **suburbs**. They need transportation systems to travel and move goods about, so there are busy roads,

CITY PROFILE

City **skyscrapers** are tall and close together. They attract wildlife that prefers high cliffs and ledges. Further out, there are bigger open spaces with trees and grasses, which are home to many more species.

waterways and railways. Drainage, sewage, and waste-disposal services are also important to keep a city clean and its inhabitants healthy.

The many different parts of a city provide **habitats**, which seem quite unlike the forests, grasslands and fields in the surrounding countryside. Yet a wide variety of animals and plants have made their homes among the closely packed buildings and hustle and bustle. As cities have grown, they have pushed out certain **species** but others have changed their behavior to suit city life. Many have found places to live that are similar to their habitats in the wild.

▼ Sydney in Australia has plenty of space and many species of wildlife in its parks and gardens.

WHERE IN THE WORLD?

Cities have been built on every **continent** except Antarctica. Most are found in **temperate** and **tropical** regions, where much of the world's food is grown. There are fewer cities in the far north and south, where the population is small because the climate is very cold.

Most cities have grown up in places which are easy to reach and have good food and water supplies.

Many were built beside rivers, on natural harbors or where rivers meet the sea. This made it easy to move goods in or out by boat and transport them to other cities nearby for trading. Settlers building a city on a foreign coastline would look for a safe, sheltered **anchorage**.

As cities have developed around the world, they have created habitats for their own groups of wildlife.

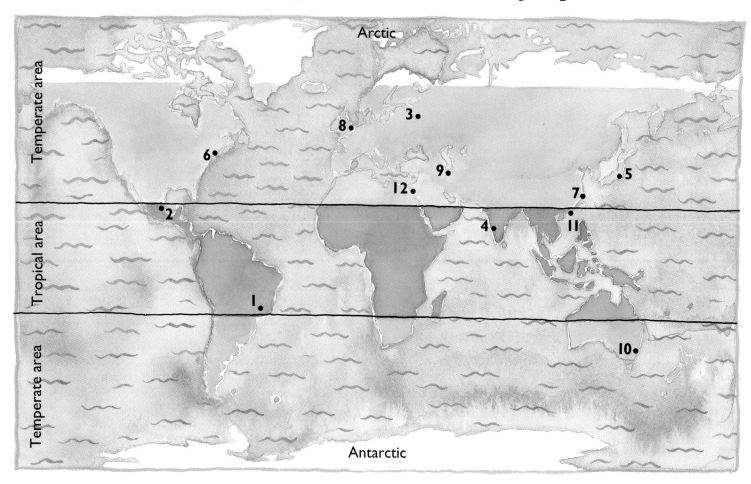

These 12 cities are among the largest in the world

1 São Paulo	4 Bombay	7 Shanghai	10 Sydney
2 Mexico City	5 Tokyo	8 London	11 Hong Kong
3 Moscow	6 New York City	9 Tehran	12 Cairo

▼ Some cities are built at the foot of mountain ranges, where land is flatter. Rio de Janeiro in Brazil sits on a natural harbor, surrounded by steep mountains.

▲ Some ancient cities, such as Carcassonne in France, were built where they could easily be defended from enemy attacks. Thick walls were built around them to give extra security.

DID YOU KNOW?

● The oldest walled city in the world is Jericho in Jordan, built around 7,800 BC.

● The northernmost capital city in the world is Reykjavik in Iceland. The capital which is furthest south is Wellington, on New Zealand's North Island. The highest city is Lhasa in Tibet, standing at 12,087 ft (3,684 m).

● City populations are difficult to measure because a city's boundaries are not always clear. Many people consider São Paulo in Brazil as the city with the highest population in the world today. It has over 10 million inhabitants.

CITY PEOPLE

Although cities have existed for centuries, they have grown much more rapidly over the past few hundred years. Now that worldwide travel is so easy, the people living in a city often come from a wide range of races and cultures. As centers of trade and industry, cities have always been among the world's wealthiest places, attracting people from the surrounding countryside looking for work and a better life.

The lifestyle of the many people who live in cities affects the air and water around them. Industry, transportation and waste-disposal systems can cause serious **pollution**. This in turn affects the wildlife that shares our noisy, crowded city centers.

DID YOU KNOW?

● The world's tallest apartment building is a 78-floor tower in New York. People live in apartments on 48 of the floors. The other floors are used as offices. The block is 716 ft (218 m) high. The tallest office building in North America is in Chicago. It has 110 floors and is 1,454 ft (443 m) high.

In some cities, many people live crowded together in run-down housing or **slums**. The poorest have shacks and huts made from materials such as odd pieces of wood and corrugated iron. These areas are known as shanty towns. They have no proper water supply or drainage. Disease spreads quickly and **pests** such as rats are common.

▼ This is Shanghai in China, one of the world's largest and busiest cities.

There is little space in most city centers. Land is very expensive and crowded. Many people live in high-rise apartments or skyscrapers with few terraces or gardens.

The majority of city dwellers live around the edge of the city, in the suburbs. Here, the land is cheaper than in the center, so houses are more spread out. They often have open spaces between them, which help to encourage many wildlife species.

◀ Apartments such as these in Singapore are packed very close together. The only place that the people can hang their washing is out of the windows.

PETS OR PESTS?

Many animals make their homes in cities. They have found the conditions ideal and now prefer the city to any other environment. Some are welcome visitors which people like to see in parks and gardens. But many have bred so rapidly that they are seen as pests and can even be a health risk to humans. Although we encourage animals such as squirrels, they can be a nuisance to us when they cause damage to our homes and our possessions.

Rodents are common in cities all over the world. Rats and mice first spread by travelling on ships from one port to another. Black rats live above ground in pipes and lofts. Brown rats prefer to be underground in drains and sewers. They feed on waste washed down from the streets.

Cracks and holes in city houses make good homes for small animals. In tropical cities these include termites, pests that gnaw wood and can cause buildings to collapse.

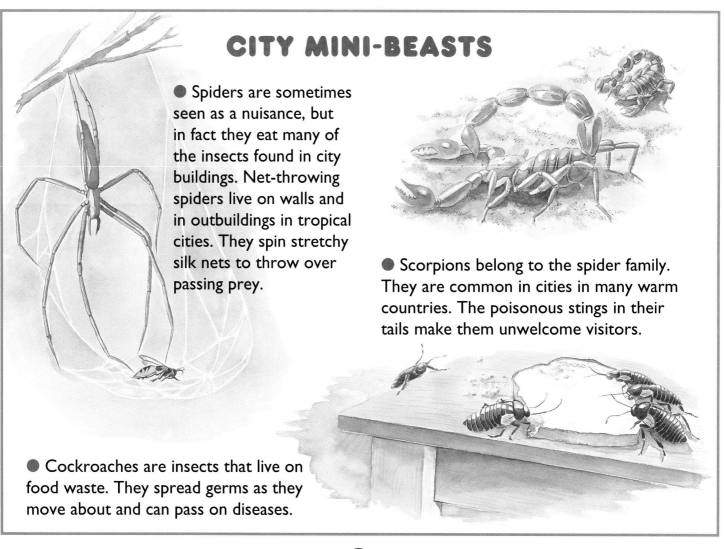

CITY MINI-BEASTS

● Spiders are sometimes seen as a nuisance, but in fact they eat many of the insects found in city buildings. Net-throwing spiders live on walls and in outbuildings in tropical cities. They spin stretchy silk nets to throw over passing prey.

● Scorpions belong to the spider family. They are common in cities in many warm countries. The poisonous stings in their tails make them unwelcome visitors.

● Cockroaches are insects that live on food waste. They spread germs as they move about and can pass on diseases.

◄ House mice have lived with people since the first cities were built. Both rats and mice can do a great deal of damage by gnawing through wires and wood. They also get into food supplies and spoil them and they can transmit diseases. In the fourteenth century, a plague called the Black Death spread across Europe. Rat fleas carried it and passed it on by biting people.

▼ Larger animals such as these raccoons usually live in a city's open areas. They come out at night to hunt through litter, overturning trash cans and leaving a trail of rubbish as they go.

STREET CREATURES

For most animals, the attraction of a city is the good supply of food that they can always find among people's trash. Many different species **scavenge** for scraps in trash cans and on garbage dumps and have **adapted** well to the city environment. Any pet food left outdoors will also encourage other hungry visitors.

In European countries, red foxes venture into gardens and parks at night. In Australia, possums can be found raiding trash cans outside houses. In some American cities there are coyotes, which belong to the wolf family. In hotter areas, such as Florida, alligators are occasionally found in people's swimming pools.

▲ In the port of Limassol in Cyprus, pelicans scavenge for fish from tourists and townspeople.

▼ In the Canadian town of Churchill, polar bears come looking for food in garbage dumps.

▶ Langurs are very common in Indian cities. They live and play in parks and gardens, along with another species of monkey called rhesus macaque. Both are very agile and can climb up walls quickly and easily. There are more monkeys living in the cities in India than in the forests.

WINTER VISITORS

In cold countries where snow often covers the ground and there is little to eat, some normally shy animals wander through suburban streets in search of food.

● Early in the morning in northern Canadian cities, mule deer, white-tailed deer, moose and elk are sometimes seen in the streets.

● On the outskirts of the Russian city of Moscow, there are European elk.

HIGH FLIERS

Many birds have adapted well to city life. Walls and roofs provide habitats which are similar to cliffs and trees and provide plenty of ledges for hunting, nesting and **roosting**. During the day, buildings absorb heat, which they release back into the air at night. They also give shelter from the wind, so cities are warmer than surrounding countryside. In winter, this attracts flocks of birds, such as starlings.

Pigeons have lived in cities since Roman times and are common all over the world. In many places, they have become a nuisance because their droppings can be a health hazard and can damage buildings.

▼ In tropical cities, weaverbirds scavenge for food among the leftovers from people's meals. Bulbuls and sunbirds are also seen in parks and gardens.

▲ A kestrel perches high on a rooftop, keeping a lookout for prey such as small birds, rodents or insects. Larger birds, such as pigeons, attract peregrine falcons to the city. Though normally mountain and coastal birds, they use tall buildings instead of rocky cliffs for their nests. They swoop down on their prey, diving at up to 180 miles (290 km) per hour. In Toronto in Canada, the peregrines have become famous and are well looked after by city people.

◀ Storks normally nest and raise their chicks in tall trees, but they sometimes use pylons, spires and chimneys. In some European cities, people have built special platforms for the storks to nest on.

GREEN STREETS

Many plants that grow in cities are different from those found in the surrounding countryside. Only a few species remain from the habitat on which the city was built. Most have either escaped from gardens, been specially planted, or are **weeds**. Weeds are often annual plants, which means that they live for only one year. They flower and their seeds grow into new plants the following year. They produce many light seeds which float easily in the air and spread widely, so they are the first plants to **colonize** bare ground. Many unusual plants have often grown from seeds brought in by ships arriving from foreign ports.

City trees must survive very harsh conditions, such as air pollution, dust and dirt from heavy traffic. Their roots are often covered by tarmac and sidewalks. The common lime and London plane are species that grow well in today's cities. Plane trees can shed their bark, getting rid of clogging soot, so that they thrive even when pollution levels are high.

◀ Mayweed and bindweed are both common on city garbage dumps and in parks and gardens. Bindweed has large, trumpet-like white flowers. Its stems twist anticlockwise around other plants, using them for support as it grows. Like another similar plant called Japanese knotweed, bindweed was once grown as an ornamental plant. It grew so fast and so well that it has become a nuisance to gardeners.

▶ Some cities have streets lined with trees, like these jacarandas in Harare, the capital of Zimbabwe. They look attractive and provide some shade in hot weather. They also give wildlife an easy route from the countryside into city centers.

THE BUTTERFLY BUSH

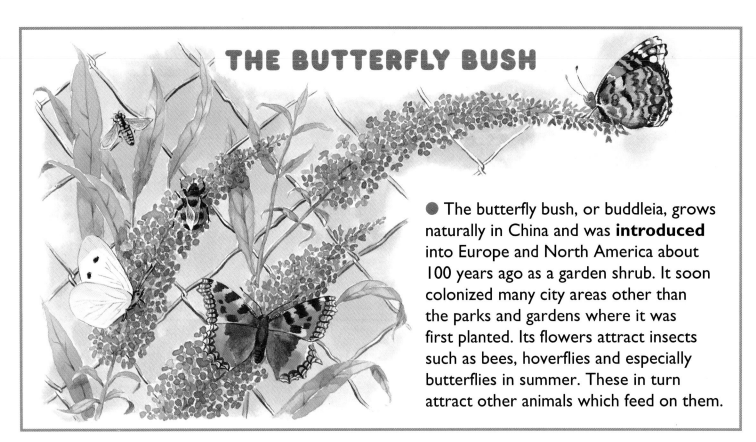

● The butterfly bush, or buddleia, grows naturally in China and was **introduced** into Europe and North America about 100 years ago as a garden shrub. It soon colonized many city areas other than the parks and gardens where it was first planted. Its flowers attract insects such as bees, hoverflies and especially butterflies in summer. These in turn attract other animals which feed on them.

OPEN SPACES

Every city has some space for leisure and recreation and to make the crowded center look more attractive. Parks and gardens provide homes for a huge variety of wildlife that would not normally be found in a city environment. Lakes, rivers, canals and other stretches of water attract species such as herons, frogs, toads and even turtles or terrapins. Some snakes like quiet corners of city parks and can be helpful to people because they prey on rats and mice.

Most cities have dumps and landfill sites where waste is dumped. Many species of rodents, insects and birds scavenge there, such as gulls, bald eagles in Alaska, and vultures and marabou storks in Africa.

▼ Central Park, in the middle of New York City, fills an area the size of 500 football fields.

◄ Areas of wasteland, disused warehouses and docks are among the open spaces found in a city. They often remain undisturbed and peaceful for long periods, so they make ideal habitats for wildlife. Plants quickly colonize wasteland and attract insects such as butterflies, which in their turn attract birds. Soon a whole community of plants and animals develops. This creates new **food chains**, with one living thing feeding off another.

NOOKS AND CRANNIES

Walls might seem unlikely habitats for wildlife, but in fact they are similar to natural cliffs and provide homes for many species. They can be made from various materials and may be in shade or full sunlight, sheltered or exposed. The best walls for wildlife are of brick or stone, with plenty of holes and crevices where small creatures can hide. There may also be rough surfaces and ledges where seeds can land and begin to grow. In warm countries, lizards and small, flat-bodied geckos run up and down walls, chasing tiny insects, or bask in the sun. Some have tiny claws to help them cling to rough surfaces, and special pads on their feet, which improve their grip.

▲ The agama lizards of Africa are found on walls and rocks and in gardens. When the male is ready to mate, he becomes very colorful and nods his head up and down to attract a female.

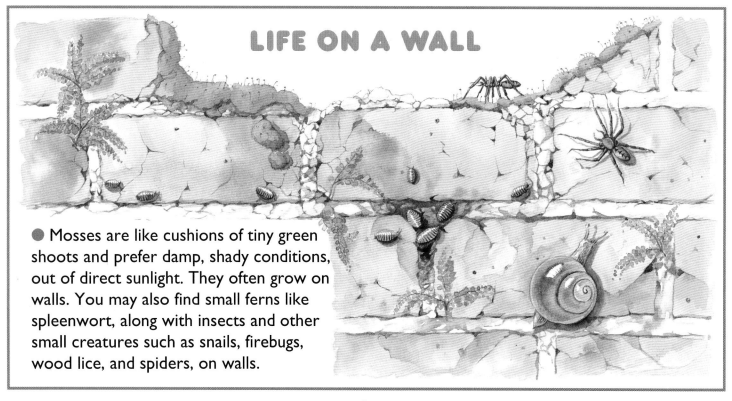

LIFE ON A WALL

● Mosses are like cushions of tiny green shoots and prefer damp, shady conditions, out of direct sunlight. They often grow on walls. You may also find small ferns like spleenwort, along with insects and other small creatures such as snails, firebugs, wood lice, and spiders, on walls.

▶ This stone statue has lichen on its surface. There are many different species of lichens and some thrive in city environments.

Lichens are plants with no leaves, roots or stems. They often grow on city walls and are made up of a fungus and a tiny plant called an alga. Scientists can use lichens to help measure the level of air pollution in cities. They are very sensitive to an invisible gas called sulphur dioxide, which is found in exhaust fumes and causes **acid rain**.

▼ Cemeteries offer peaceful habitats to a wide variety of plants and animals on and around the gravestones and walls. They are important open spaces, sometimes dating back hundreds of years.

SPREADING CITIES

City wildlife is under threat. Open spaces and wasteland are being used for building, as land becomes scarcer and more expensive. This is pushing out the plants and animals that live there, and many of those that remain are being harmed by air pollution. Yet habitats in every environment are constantly changing. Just as land may be cleared for development, so a tree may fall in a forest and widlife has to adapt to these changes. Some species are lost but others soon replace them.

City planners have learned that trees are not just attractive homes for wildlife. They also work like small air conditioners, because water evaporates from the surface of their leaves during the day, cooling the air around them. In some cities, people are cleaning up their local areas and encouraging wildlife by creating **nature preserves** to protect it. These can also help us to learn more about what we can do for the future of life in the cities.

◀ One way of encouraging the city wildlife we like to see is to put out bird feeders or nesting boxes. This Mexican hummingbird would usually drink nectar from flowers.

Planners are improving city environments by introducing greenery and open spaces. Hanging or creeping plants cover walls, and some buildings have roof gardens with ponds, flower beds and even trees.

▼ This public garden is a welcome green area in the crowded city of Tokyo, Japan. Land there is very expensive and scarce and is normally used for building, rather than for open spaces.

CITY ACTION

● Use public transportion whenever you can (or better still, bicycle or walk) instead of going by car.

● Don't forget that litter can harm wildlife. Dispose of it carefully and make sure you recycle as much paper and as many bottles and cans as possible.

● Visit local parks and gardens and see how many kinds of wildlife you can spot. Support your local nature preserves.

● If you live in the city center, you can attract some species to your windowsill or balcony by putting out bird food or growing plants that attract insects such as butterflies.

CUZCO – FIRST CITY OF THE INCAS

For thousands of years, people have told stories about the world around them. Often these stories try to explain something that people do not really understand, such as how the world began or where light comes from. This is a tale from Peru about the Incas and how they built their first city.

A very long time ago, before there was a sun or moon or stars, the great god Viracocha created the world. First he made light and from it he created the sun, moon and stars. After this, he carved human figures out of stone. He painted them and then breathed life into them. He made animals too and gave them life, but the people were most special to him. Before leaving them on the shores of Lake Titicaca, he told them, "Never forget me. Worship me always." But they forgot.

Viracocha created other gods to watch over the people. Inti Illapa, the thunder god, sent down rain to make the land fertile. Huallallo, the god of fire, and Pariacaca, the god of water, kept the Earth warm. But they were always fighting one another, so the land was either too hot or too cold, depending upon who was winning. The stars watched over everything that had been created, but the greatest protector of all was Inti, the sun god, brother of Mamaquilla, the moon.

The great sun god looked down upon the wild people of the Earth, who lived in caves and fed on roots and berries. He felt sorry for them.

He decided to send one of his sons, named Ayar Manco, to teach the people how to make tools, farm the land, and build places to live.

He called for his son and said to him, "I have a task for you. Look at these poor, wild people on Earth. Go among them and teach them how to live peacefully."

"But how shall I do this?" asked Ayar Manco.

"You must help them build a great city where they can live together and prosper. In the heart of the city they must build a temple in honor of me," the sun god replied. Then he gave his son a golden rod. "Take this with you," he said. "When the rod sinks easily into the soil, you will have found the right place to build their city."

So Ayar Manco set off, wearing his golden robes and magnificent jewels. He carried with him the special golden rod from his father.

When he arrived at Lake Titicaca, the wild people saw him glittering in the early morning sun and bowed down to worship their new god.

"Follow me," he told them. "I will lead you to a new and better life."

Ayar Manco searched for many days for a good place to build the city. Every day the wild people

watched as he tried to push the golden rod into the soil. But he had no success. Ayar Manco was beginning to lose hope. At last, he arrived at a beautiful valley with high mountains towering on either side of it. Here the golden rod sank easily into the rich soil.

"We have found the place to build our city! But first we must start work on a great temple in honor of my father," Ayar Manco announced to the wild people.

They were eager to begin, but work was almost impossible because of the strong wind that was howling through the valley.

"Please help us, Ayar Manco," they cried. "We are trying as hard as we can, but we can hardly carry these stones and the dust is blowing into our eyes and hurting us."

Ayar Manco managed to catch the wind in a cave, rolling a huge rock across the entrance to trap it.

"Now you can get on with your work in peace," he told the people.

But no sooner had they finished building the temple than Ayar Manco's brother arrived and saw that the wind had been imprisoned. He was furious.

"How could you do this to my friend!" he yelled, and he vowed to release the wind at sunset.

Ayar Manco knew that it was impossible to finish building the whole city before sunset, so he made another plan. He caught the sun as it passed over the mountain tops and tied it to a high rock so that it could not set. Ayar Manco did not let the sun and wind go until the very last stone was laid in the city.

And that was how Cuzco, the first city of the Incas, was built. Ayar Manco decided to stay among the people he had grown close to. He changed his name to Manco Capac and became the first ruler of the mighty Inca Empire.

TRUE OR FALSE?

*Which of these facts are true and which ones are false?
If you have read this book carefully, you will know the answers.*

1. Cities are found on every continent.

2. Mosses like damp, shady places.

3. Raccoons are nighttime visitors to gardens in Australia.

4. Black rats are found in city drains and sewers.

5. A plague called the Black Death was spread by cockroaches.

6. Scavengers eat food waste.

7. A langur is a type of monkey.

8. Pigeons have lived in cities for more than 2,000 years.

9. An annual plant only lives for 12 months.

10. The butterfly bush comes from North America.

11. Trees can cool the air.

12. The bald eagle can be spotted in garbage dumps in Australia.

13. The largest city in the world is New York City.

GLOSSARY

● **Acid rain** When the air has been polluted by gases from industry and vehicle engines, they turn rain into a weak acid. It can damage lakes, trees, and buildings.

● **Adapt** To change behavior or form to suit the local conditions.

● **Anchorage** A safe place where a ship can put down its anchor.

● **Colonize** When wildlife begins to live or grow in a place where none already lives, it colonizes the area.

● **Continent** A very large island or area of mainland, usually divided into a number of countries.

● **Environment** The conditions that exist in the place where an animal or plant lives, including the air, water, climate, other animals and plants.

● **Food chain** A natural chain in which energy is passed between living things. For example, rabbits eat grass, foxes eat rabbits, and so on.

● **Habitat** The natural home of an animal or plant.

● **Introduce** To bring a species into an area where it does not occur naturally.

● **Nature preserve** An area where plants and animals are protected by law.

● **Pests** Troublesome animals that occur in large numbers and often cause damage.

● **Pollution** The release into the environment of harmful substances that damage or poison living things.

● **Population** The total number of people, animals or plants living in a particular area.

● **Rodents** Small mammals, such as rats and mice, which have strong front teeth for gnawing hard objects.

● **Roosting** A bird roosts when it rests on a ledge or branch at night.

● **Scavengers** Animals that feed on the dead bodies of other animals.

● **Skyscrapers** Tall buildings with many floors.

● **Slums** Overcrowded areas of cities with very poor housing.

● **Species** A group of animals or plants that share the same characteristics and can breed with each other.

● **Suburbs** Areas around the edge of a town or city with more housing and less industry than in the center.

● **Temperate** The areas of the world that lie between the hot tropics and the cold poles. The climate in temperate countries varies with the seasons.

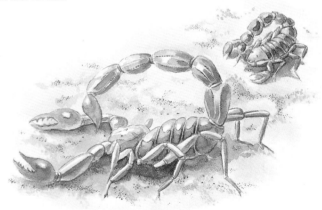

● **Trade** To buy and sell goods.

● **Tropics** The very hot, wet areas of the world that lie either side of the Equator.

● **Weeds** Plants that grow quickly and easily in places where they are not wanted.

INDEX

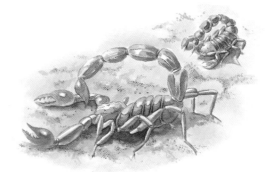